The Blue Room Anthology

editors:
Lisa Matthews
Sheila Mulhern
Ellen Phethean
Jane Wood

First published 1999 by:
Diamond Twig
5 Bentinck Road
Newcastle upon Tyne
NE4 6UT
Tel/fax 0191 273 5326
email: poetics@nildram.co.uk

Typeset in Palatino in 11pt

Printed by Peterson Printers, South Shields

ISBN 0 9520090 5 6

Diamond Twig acknowledges
the financial assistance
of Northern Arts

The Blue Room is supported by New Writing North
and Newcastle City Council

Contents

The History of The Blue Room

It was the brain-child of Ellen Phethean. A discussion took place between Ellen, Lisa Matthews and I where the idea was put forward.

'A venue where new women writers can read their work.'

'A friendly and supportive atmosphere.'

'And a new type of audience - people who wouldn't normally go to such an event, people who would feel awkward at an "Arts" venue.'

'An informal setting.'

'A pub.'

'But the work that is read must be of a high standard.'

It was agreed. And when Gillian Allnutt came up with the name, The Blue Room was born.

Following a grant of £450.00 from New Writing North the first meeting took place in April 1997 at The Frog and Nightgown pub in Newcastle. The format was that on the first Sunday of the month 4 readers (usually 2 poets and 2 prose writers) read for 10-15 minutes each and received a fee of £10.00. The format has remained the same but the venue has changed to The Head of Steam pub (opposite Newcastle Central Station). Twenty meetings have taken place since The Blue Room's inception with an average audience of thirty.

The readers are women, but the audience is mixed and we have included three successful "men's nights" amongst the twenty sessions. There has also been a "swapping genres" night when established writers wrote in unfamiliar genres and read the results to a packed Blue Room.

In 1997 The Blue Room was shortlisted for a Northern Electric Arts Award.

In 1998 we received a grant of £500.00 from Newcastle City Council which enabled us to continue for a second year.

In 1999 a highly successful event was held at the Live Theatre. John Hegley, who had expressed admiration for The Blue Room concept, agreed to come to Newcastle to perform along with The Poetry Virgins in a Valentine's Day special.

The Blue Room has become well established as part of the Newcastle literary scene. And we have added a fourth member, Sheila Mulhern, to our organising team.
In April 1999 we widened its scope by starting a writing workshop that is held each month before The Blue Room reading. This is aimed at women who are not yet at the stage of being potential Blue Room readers, and also women who have not written before and want help getting started. We felt many of the people sending submissions to The Blue Room were writing in isolation and the workshop would be a place where they could come together with like-minded people and receive encouragement and constructive criticism of their work. The group will run initially for ten monthly sessions culminating in a celebratory performance of new writing in April 2000.

We are hoping that the Community Photography Group based at the Centre Against Unemployment in Newcastle will design and produce a series of postcards depicting some of the writing produced by the group alongside eye-catching images. This will generate interest in the writing and give the work a wider audience.

Through the writing group we hope to reach further out into the community by offering "taster" writing workshops to women's and girls' groups with a view to encouraging those interested to join The Blue Room writing group and attend the readings.

In these ways, and others yet to be thought of, we will carry on promoting women's writing and seeking out its audience.

Jane Wood. May 1999.

Foreword by John Hegley, May 1999

A great variety of voices. The room may be blue but there's a lot of other colours in it. Not enough dogs though.

On the Valentine's Day Special The Poetry Virgins ran a "Love is ..." competition. John asked us to add these to the anthology:

> Love is a four lettered word, an excellent notion, a romantic myth, a disappointed mister.
>
> Love is meaningful sex,
> like fulfilling poetry,
> requires subtlety in using
> a tongue that may or may not
> be familiar to you
>
> Love is all you need - John Lennon
>
> Love is better with a red setter (lying quietly by the fireplace)
>
> Love is O Elvis mixed up
>
> Love is a bourgeois deviation
> Love is rarely discussed in the New Scientist
>
> Love is a man who comes and then goes
>
> Love is not grimacing when he comes straight up and kisses you before he wipes his mouth
> on the inside of your thigh
>
> Love is canny, love is shrewd, love is very very rude
>
> Love Viz ? yes, especially Billy the Fish
>
> Love is like a violin, sometimes out, sometimes in (Ken Dodd)
>
> Love is, isn't it ?

Extract

Andrea Badenoch

Outside, the exit road curved away like a dark snake. Jazz needed to hitch a lift but felt reluctant to face the night. She picked up her bag and stepped out into the warm wind.

She crossed the carpark. A mother and father unloaded two sleeping toddlers from the back of a Ford Escort. Jazz noted their roof rack loaded with luggage and their window stickers showing previous holiday destinations. She thought of her own family and of Peony and Mimosa and how they'd never been anywhere apart from Redcar sands. I'm going home, she thought to herself.

She walked past the petrol station and down the slip road towards the motorway's convoy of lorries, its buzz of anxious cars. I'm going home, she thought again.

She turned around. The family with the sleeping children entered the service station. It shone like a friendly island in the sea of night. Jazz stood on the grass verge, hesitated, then loosened her hair, letting the wind stir it around her face. She felt smaller than ever in the darkness. She stood casually for a moment, her thin hip jutting, then she stretched out her arm.

A car stopped immediately. It was a new Mondeo, red and throaty. It throbbed lustily at her side. The driver leant over and opened both the passenger and the rear door. There was a blare of music. She threw her bag on the back seat then climbed in next to him. As she clipped together her seatbelt he turned down the volume of the CD. Jazz saw that he was about twenty seven, smart and smelling of scent. He smiled, accelerated and cruised over into the sparse but fast moving outside lane.

Jazz inspected his suit, his gleaming collar, a faint shadow on his jaw, a nervous pulse in his temple.

"Michael," he said. "I'm only going as far as Cambridge."

Jazz smiled and took off Fat Andy's driving gloves. She turned round and tucked them into her sports bag. She recognised his flat friendly accent. He was from Leeds.

"Call me Mike," he added self-consciously. "I'm from Leeds."

Jazz decided at that moment she could do with a bit of short term help from Mike.

She was in no hurry and she was tired. In an instant she had assessed

both Mike's affluence and his susceptibility. He's not a weirdo, she thought to herself. He's ordinary and safe. He won't give me any trouble.
"Hi Mike," she replied, moving closer, placing her right arm behind his head rest in a gesture that was both innocent and seductive.
With a roar from the engine he overtook a BMW. He was trying to impress her.
Jazz decided he was a good driver but not as good as Fat Andy and definitely not as good as herself. He took a cigarette out of a packet on his lap and pressed the dashboard lighter. "It's a dangerous game," he said, "thumbing lifts." He inhaled.
There was a silence. "Do you always travel this way then?"
Jazz adopted a slightly breathless tone It was one she'd sometimes used with Andy when she wanted her own way. She exaggerated her northern accent. "Only with nice lads. Nice lads with decent cars." She sounded at least six years younger than she actually was. She sounded under-age.
He changed gear and his hand brushed her knee.
He pretended it was an accident.
"That's all right," Jazz murmured softly.

What Is Worth Knowing
after Sujata Bhatt

Celia McCulloch

(This poem first appeared in Iron magazine)

That bread in its bowl breeds
needs nurture in the dark and warmth.
That she could die and neighbours not know,
the child keening at her side.
That not only bread breeds –
beer too needs kindness to brew,
healing hands and sleep.
That you must bow and beg pardon
of an elder before you cut.
That you can burn ash green
but not oak or sycamore.
That bread and beer breed
in kindness and yogurt too:
hold your finger in the milk and count to twenty –
if you are not burnt your yogurt will live
or your beer or bread.
That the same applies to kindred wool or silk –
dip your elbow in and bath them like babies.
That Mozart feeds the mind
which also is a baby.
That untouched, even pearls die.

Summerhill Square
Newcastle Westend 1991

Celia McCulloch
(This poem first appeared in Iron magazine)

Autumn is bonfires, marbles, smoke – Elizabeth Jennings

Six o'clock and the air is delicate gauze,
the street serenely empty. Scent of smoke
drifts down from Elswick Road, Ryehill Estate,
where lads do handbrake turns, intimidate
the frail behind doors shut against the choke
of burning Fords and gallery applause.

And here outside the ring of devilment
the park is green, yet smoke came coiling
last night, let loose, groping down the hill
like an uncorked genie out for a kill.
Then pulled up short, parole revoked, crawling,
it veered and sloped back home impenitent.

Tonight on the street the evening air
smells nostalgic, like bonfires, feels like war.

A Sea Change

Vera Kulkarni

First light embroiders the north quay.
Its needles trace cobbles, footsteps
with threads of pink, aquamarine.
Fishing boats wreathed in cobwebs,
fly-stitched, reach for the open sea.

Fingers of light touch the windows,
scratch a surface of shellac.
The *'Lazy Daisy '* and trawlers,
hemmed in a harbour, sea-fret
on the awakening river.

White spinnakers flap in the breeze.
Her long hair clipped in French knots
and the look in her eyes sea-green,
Mother's worked into sackcloth.
She's filleting mackerel at Shields.

A fresh wind is feathering surf,
fronds of kelp, withered sea-pinks,
herring bones and kippered earth.
The colliers' rust but dust has wings
where rigs and North Sea ferries berth.

Another season, a neap tide,
a sea-change brings a new day.
Clamouring waves chew at the Groyne,
nibble at Marsden Rock, the Bay,
feed on the hunger of the Tyne.

A Night in the Country

Vera Kulkarni

We slapped the sun like butter in the dairy,
stashed the harvest moon in a granary;
kepped the midnight moth in a nightjar.

We plodged the darkness of water to the pollards
where the wild deer lipped the bark of willow.
Unruly briars grabbed my legs, tore the skin.

We rushed home, snecked the door, slammed the bolt in.
Later, indulged in after-dinner chatter,
caresses, camaraderie, banter.

Carafes of wine flowed under the canopy.
A barn owl flew into our company
and left with the silence of a hunter.

We necked the sky and mapped the North Star.
Screeches stabbed into the night, split the mood.
Sounds like the torments of Hell. Blue murder.

We tracked the noise and found two bundles of fur,
the blood red claws of scrapping badgers.
We yelled them apart. Snuffed out the candles.

Motherhood

Debbie Taylor

I hated to let her go. Out into the wom-world to get her child. To the clinic where the cutter works – I warned her what he'd do to her. But she was determined to be like the others.

"Don't fuss, animata!" Once it was decided she was impatient to be gone. "He must do hundreds of operations every year. And it's so quick now, and painless – not like when you were young."

I know she's right, that everyone has their daughters done these days. But all I could think of was her glorious thick hair; of the honeyed weight of it in my hands as I plaited it each morning, the way it would slide through my fingers.

The posters make it seem so simple, the cutting: the precise circle shaved; the skin peeled back in a red flap. And the laser's almost silent now, they say. They can get the lobe out with almost no bruising.

Afterwards, she said it was nice to be allowed to walk in the sun again. The malls were crammed with woms, she said, with scarves knotted under their chins and changing-bags on the handles of their buggies.

And I suppose it will be nice to have a child around the place again. Though you've no control, these days, of what you'll get. They took the labels off the spermessaries years ago. Not that she cares. Since she was cut, she's been all titmilk and tenderness. The child could be a grunt-clone for all she knows, soused with testosterone: a brick-hodder or khaki-strutter; factory fodder.

This morning, when I was pinning up her hair – you know, wrapping it around to cover the bald patch – she smiled up at me with her stupid vacant eyes. "Thank you, animata," she said. "Thank you for letting me go." I had to leave the room. I pretended I needed more hairpins.

Thursday – Extract

Betty Weiner

When I set off it was no different from any other Thursday except the bus didn't come so I walked.

I didn't recognize the counter assistant and she pushed my change under the glass without speaking. Sometimes they say "Is it still raining?" or I say "Pretty busy, is it?". But not today. Going down to the basement I noticed the stairs were dusty. The attendant was somewhere else and the signing-in book wasn't visible so I undressed and sat in one of the hot rooms. Then I went into the steam room.

Then I showered and rested. The jacuzzi was out of order. It irritates me when the jacuzzi's not working.

In the swimming pool the water was chilly. It happens from time to time – engineering problems or a blitz on costs. I did my twenty lengths, slipped my costume off in the changing room, wrapped myself in my big towel and headed back for the Turkish Suite. When I got downstairs the Turkish Suite had disappeared. Grit on the corridor floor scratched under my canvas shoes. A heap of matted dust in one corner looked like a crouching insect. The door to the Turkish rooms was half open and I could see frayed rope and two or three overturned chairs. Another room, further down the corridor, was locked. There was a faded rectangle of paint where the name of the room should have been. Half an hour ago it said SAUNA. All that remained of the public telephone was a chipped hood. It was like being in a disaster area. I went back up to the reception area in my towel. The attendant didn't remember selling me a ticket an hour ago and said the Turkish Suite had been closed for years. I said my bag was there and my clothes. She said they couldn't be. I said I left them in a locker. She said the lockers had been sold when the Turkish and Sauna facilities closed. Did I wish to look in the Lost Property drawer? She opened a drawer and held up a hand towel and several sets of swimming goggles. I rejected the lost property and asked for the Manager. The attendant pointed to a Complaints Box near the exit. When I turned back to the counter she was already taking money from the next customer. I said, "Just a minute - " and from nowhere two pool guards appeared and propelled me out of the building. I didn't know what to do so I headed for home. As I turned into the High Street I was surprised to see mounted police in riot gear outside the entrance to the shopping precinct. Because of the horses I couldn't at first see what they were guarding but as I came nearer I thought I could see – under the horses' bellies and between one horse and another – children. I crossed the road and saw that the police were guarding young teenage children, mostly boys but also a few girls, who were fastened to hooks in the walls of the buildings by devices rather like bicycle locks. Each child had an arm or a foot fastened to the wall, depending on the position of the hook. I had seen dogs fastened to walls like this. As I watched two vans with the words "ORDER (Truant Collection)" and a logo like an academic cap appeared and some clean shaven men wearing heavy boots with very shiny toecaps jumped out.

The Alien Concept Of A Woman My Age Rollerblading

Philippa Collingwood

From pushchairs I get
It's a lady.
From my peer and gender group
How brave!
Dogs rush up barking.
A mixed group of ten year olds
have stopped laughing, pointing
by my fourth glide past.

What you doin' that for? from a boy
Are you trying to keep fit? A girl.
Yes, but, also
why should kids have all the fun?
One of the older girls turns
Yeh ! Girl Power!
They're behind me now.
I raise my thumb
out of my wrist guard.

Instructions For Rollerblading

Philippa Collingwood

Bend your knees,
lean slightly forward,
relax into it
and go with the flow.
It's a glide,
nice long slides
from side to side
with a swing from the hips
never mind that the rear
sticks out, it's the rhythm
that counts till a piece of
grit under the wheels
lurches you,
jars the stomach,
flails the arms.

Like last night
between silk sheets
when your hand slid
over my smooth breast
and tripped
on the lump.

R&R

Pauline Plummer

How you watched me through your night sight – spilling
the beans, this is my life, dared me to care –
my gander in black and tan abseiling
in from Aran, sparrow hawks in your hair.

Your bite was soft as gas. You liked worn
out glamour, seductive and maternal
to press your bony frame against, again,
again. To hell with any scandal.

You were all speed and half rations fasting
to be hard, to survive Belfast, the Gulf,
the swamps of Belize – danger wasting
your capacity to love – sex was enough.

I watched you on the bay, breathing in stars,
running towards excitement, towards war.

Buying a Blouse That Fits

Pauline Plummer

The streets are wrapped
in old newspapers to keep warm.
Reflected in ice we see
a black girl with a shaved head
vomiting into a bin.

The Thai waitress gives you
one of those are you pleased with my smile smiles
and after coffee
the manager asks you
do you want boys or girls?
Ah the English are so cold, no.
We drink warm beer
while ghosts in the juke box
serenade our broken faith.

You have frost in your hair.
Have I aged? I ask.
I lie about my size
but you buy me a blouse that fits, anyway.
In the train the couple opposite
tear into each other
like a trapped bear biting off its paw.
Later in the hotel
you try my skin against yours for size.

Inter-railing

Ally May
(First published in Blissed-out for 5 Neruda Press)

I don't regret going inter-railing
in Heworth,
the blossom was out
I don't regret feeling guilty about the dog's ribs
in the kitchen in 87
scuffing my shoes on the way home from school
or wanting more drama
on weekdays,
I don't regret riding my bike
through puddles in the back lane,
wanting to go out drinking
wanting to go out drinking all the time
going down to the dene as the trees swayed
in the pale sky,
I don't regret pouring hot water on you
for saying
you wouldn't want black people in your family.

Lionhead

Ally May

we took a train to the bay
she was herself
in the blazing sunshine
that I could taste in my mouth
her sunglasses matched her lips
there was no trace of clouds
the water like windows
counting pebbles, she laughed, told me
listen to the breeze coast across the shore
listen to the waves turning back into water

Tuesday Morning

Ally May

A sunny day
I'm walking near Two Ball Lonnen
with a headache and a sore foot
from Tilley's cheese and pate bar last night.
There is a slight breeze
I've got no plans for later.
If you think about justice
it doesn't make you happy.

The Capital Of Know Your Place

Ally May

First thing in the morning you look so beautiful
or at least I bet you do
rain makes silver sparks when it hits the ground.
Karifa and Karifa's kids are walking through the streets.
This Newcastle. The bomb.
This Friday night feeling.
I try to remember the days I was only bored to tears.

Tired And Looking At Streetlights

Ally May

sometimes I feel no one would notice me
if I turned up in their bath
it looks as if my dog is dead now
the video broke in a street in beacon lough
we danced in the mist on the way from the pub
add the good times to the bad
what are you left with ?

Buttons and Braces

June Portlock

I'm looking for a man
with buttoned-up flies.
You see, I know that men really seem to go
for wanton states of undress in women.
Basque, suspenders, garters, stockings,
so

I'm looking for a man
with braces.
Snappy!

He could slip them off his shoulders
slowly,
or undo the front
and fling
them behind him all abandoned.

They tell me I'm an old-fashioned girl
so

I'm looking for a man
with sock suspenders.
After he undid them, and peeled off
his raglan patterned pure botany wool,
he could leave them,

dangling.

Oh yes!
That's what I'm looking for.

First Collection, 'Broken Biscuits', Diamond Twig 1997

Dear Milkman

June Portlock

Dear Milkman,

I thought that when two pints arrived yesterday
that one
was for the day before, that's yesterday's yesterday
but it was for the next day - that's today
you'd brought a pint for tomorrow without
leaving a pint for today -
that's the day before yesterday,
so I am one pint short.

However,
you did remember to bring the extra one
I asked for last week this time which
I didn't pay for
because I thought you would forget,
like you always forget to shut the gate.
So the one you did bring equals the other one
that you didn't bring the other day,
that's not yesterday but the day before.

Will you be coming for payment tomorrow,
or later today?
Not last week, or the week before but the week
before that you didn't come.
I know this because the gate was shut.
But on the next week, that's the week before last,
you collected the week before lasts and
the week before the week before lasts together.

Last week this time you came yesterday.
I was out yesterday, but I don't think you came
because the gate was shut
and the week before that it was tomorrow,
but I'm definitely out tomorrow
so today would be best. I'm in today.

Yours sincerely
number 28.

P.S. Don't forget to shut the gate.

First published, first collection 'Broken Biscuits' Oct 1997

A Thin Line of Blood – Extract

Pat Stevens

It became a form of ceremony. In her bedroom Shona takes a razor blade out of the packet. She arranges a handful of tissues and a large Elastoplast on the desk. Then slowly, carefully, she draws the razor blade across her forearm. The pain is not immediate. It begins slowly, as the blood wells out of the thin red line. She lets the blood trickle down her arm, mopping it from the back of her hand with the tissues. The pain burns up her arm now. She begins to cry. After a short time she covers the cut with the Elastoplast. Then nursing her aching arm she curls up on her bed and cries till she sleeps.

Shona stands outside the garage waiting for her mother to give her a lift to school. This was once the best bit of the day. On the journey into town she would plan out the things she had to do. She would save little bits of gossip for her friends. She can remember looking forward to games lessons. She can remember running in her pale blue T-shirt and blue hockey skirt, lifting her stick and hitting the ball. The satisfying thud she felt in her hands and wrists. Now she climbs into the car beside her mother and sits staring blankly out of the window. At some point, she thinks, her mother is going to notice. But it won't be this morning. Because the traffic is bad, and she's running late, and she has an important meeting with a new designer, who has a range of sportswear her customers will be willing to die for. She tells Shona this as she drives.

She explains that this is why she has to drop Shona at the bus stop, instead of taking her all the way to school. Shona stands at the bus stop for about five minutes, then she crosses the road and takes the bus in the other direction. It takes her a long time to get home, because she has to change buses. She hasn't the energy to walk directly from one bus stop to the other, instead she sits on a bench in the town and watches the people rushing by her.

At home she goes upstairs to her bedroom and collapses onto the bed. When Shona asked to have her room painted white her mother was shocked. She'd expected maybe dark blue, maybe black, that was what teenagers did to rooms. Shona's room with its pure white walls, white bedspread and curtains, its stripped pine floor and its white rug is somehow deviant. Shona knows black would have killed her. She has thrown out her razor blades because the idea of cutting straight down the vein in her wrist kept coming back to her.

She lies on the bed watching the light change on the ceiling. She has no idea how long she lies there. Time has become very erratic. Sometimes she glances at her watch after a long time and finds only a minute has passed. Sometimes whole afternoons can pass without her noticing. The light on the ceiling is always changing. Sometimes it darkens, the bright lines of sunlight fade away, only to creep back slowly. Then the whole room becomes suffused in pink. The pink glow has disappeared and darker blue shadows have begun to appear when she hears her mother come home from work, hears her closing the bedroom door and moving around in the bedroom. She knocks on Shona's door.

"You OK?" she asks. Shona grunts. Her mother takes this as *yes*.

"I'm going to the gym," she says. "There's loads of salad and stuff in the fridge. Help yourself. Dad's got a meeting, he's going to eat out."

Ceasefire

Jadwiga Billewicz

Ilsa is kneading dough.
Pressing, folding,
pressing.

It will
be covered in crisp clean linen;
it will
rise, plump, in the basin.

But not yet. For now,

she is pressing, folding,
pressing, folding.
The outside into the inside,
the inside in.

Ilsa is baking a house.
Pressing, folding.

It will
be draped in the finest linen;
it will
rise, fragrant, from rubble.

But for now,

she is pressing, pressing;
folding the inside in.
Needing the outside out..

Icicle Chains

Jadwiga Billewicz
(This poem was first published in Rialto and The Nerve Anthology)

We have winters here. The snow is not
Deep. The wind
Is cut with salt. I'd never seen the sea
Then
We skated on thick ice. Rolled
Soft in drifts I was warm
With brothers
Then
Not here.

We have garlands here. Draperies breathless
With colour
Freeze the air. I'd never seen the North
Then
We inhaled orchards. Gathering
Fragrant juices I was warm
With brothers
Then
Not here.

Defrosting my Fridge

Jackie Hardy

Regular as hurricanes it happens.
Like terminal moraine from some unmapped glacier
a great white mass heaves aside
the door, threatens to engulf the kitchen.
I remove all food; turn out an ancient
jar in which there grows an exquisite mould
whose culture could save humankind or form
the base of economic rocket fuel.
Then begins the ritual of water;
slow-moving ceremonial parade
of steaming trays designed to spread the thaw,
back and forth from fridge to sink to kettle.
Soon the floor's awash with drippings; the sink
filled with ribbed icebergs large enough to hold
their shape all day.

I notice, perfectly
preserved in ice, the body of a fly;
its legs outstretched; lacy wings poised for flight;
surprised by unseasonable weather.
I consider carbon dating. This might
reveal matters pertinent to science;
but could lead to endless social surveys,
government reports, questions in the House,
headline in a tabloid – *Poets' Fridge*
Pose Hazards To Channel Shipping.
Perhaps I'll keep it secret it's been an eon
since my fridge's last defrosting.

Shoot-Out at Three Thirty

Jackie Hardy

The kitchen fills with swagger,
saloon bar truculence.
They eye my greeting like an obscene gesture,
reply in groans.

Food humanises them enough
to level at my head
their fully-loaded wants,
half-cocked ideals.

When the stampede slows
they loll in lazy esses,
await the bare-back noes,
then outlaw to music in their rooms.

Bruised, but not blooded,
I polish up my badge,
long for a shot of red-eye
and to ride, alone, into the sunset.

Break Ups

Kathy Kenny

When did it happen?

The first kiss –
we held our breath,
counted sixty in our heads –
felt like death.

When did it happen?

The second date –
the noise when he chewed
that monkey gland steak.

When did it happen?

That walk in the sand,
the way he showed off –
those stupid hand-stands.

When did it happen?

He cut like a knife –
Do you want to be a virgin
all your life?
Not forever, I said,
But definitely tonight!

When did it happen?

Nine-forty-five on the homeward bus –
his mother would worry,
he had to rush!

When did it happen?

They bumped into each other
at the bar of The Grand,
she spilled his drink –
he licked her hand.

When did it happen?

I couldn't resist –
had my hand on his knee,
forgot about my husband
on the other side of me.

When did it happen?

Flying in from Barcelona,
over snow covered Alps,
the breathtaking beauty –
our silence like ice.

Reel

Kathy Kenny

Imagine us
In hard shoes,
Skidding scuffed ankles
Across polished floors,
Sliding on
The ship's deck
Wet with whisky.

Imagine us cruising,
Curled in feather boas,
Tight gold dresses,
Sipping cocktails
One step from the edge –
The men cupping cigarettes
Against the wind.

Dying to be Tall – Extract

Liz King

Nigel switched off the electric saw and laid it down on the table. Bending over, he examined his handiwork carefully.

The corpse stared back at him, comically squinting through tufts of hair, like a clown in a circus. Its hair and scalp were pulled aside, exposing the white dome of the cranium. Running full circle around the cranium was Nigel's handiwork. A groove sawn right through the bone, down to the brain beneath.

Satisfied that the groove was complete, Nigel grasped hold of the top of the cranium and pulled. It came away from the remainder of the head, like the top off a boiled egg.

The dead brain lay naked in front of him. He eased its soft folds gently to one side until he could see the brain stem and spinal cord beneath. Reaching down with a knife, he sliced through their white flesh and then, supporting it with both hands, he lifted the brain cleanly out of the skull and laid it on the table, next to the saw.

With the brain out of the way, the inside of the cranium looked bare. Nigel reached inside and probed around the floor of the gaping cavity with his fingers until he found his target. With a delicate pair of bone cutters he snipped through a thin sheet of bone at the base of the cranium to reveal a small, juicy cherry.

"Bingo!" exclaimed Nigel. "Another little beauty."

Carefully, he lifted the pituitary gland out of the corpse and dropped it into a beaker of saline.

Golem

(A mythical creature in Jewish legend)
Ivy Hudson

Sterilised

that was considered best,
now I roam the streets
unable to understand
the meaning of love,
compassion and acceptance.

A loveless life
ignored by parents too busy to bother,
I mechanically
go through the motions
timid, afraid of my shadow.

I may as well be made of clay.

Sometimes they put me away
with others,
to stabilise, they say.
Then I am released
to start
the downward spiral again.

I can only travel in one direction.

The spirit breathed and I was formed
to live in an eddy of self-destruction.
Labelled, and despised
I lash out at the world
but the net closes in, tight.

The Band

Ivy Hudson

Bored at Sunday School
she'd tied an elastic band tightly
round and round her finger

A frantic teacher had to cut it
to restore the blood supply

Now a tight band of fears
stretches round her head

her imagination swollen

the thin gold band ever tighter

Everything You Ever Wanted to Know About Self-Mutilation (But Were Afraid to Ask) – Extract

Tracey Sinclair

The first, and most important step, is finding the right blade. This, of course, depends on exactly what it is you wish to do to yourself; for superficial marks without too much risk of scarring, an everyday kitchen knife is usually sufficient, though there is some debate as to whether a straight or serrated edge is best. A general rule is that straight tend to be sharper and will give a cleaner cut, although apparently – I say apparently because this has never been a method I favour – the hacking motion required with a serrated edge can be very satisfying. Personally, I always go for the razor blade. This is for several reasons: while the razor will almost always leave a scar, it is quite a small and neat one and, also, I am never completely convinced that kitchen knives are clean. After all, sitting cutting yourself with a knife your mother has just used to carve the Sunday roast seems more than a little unhygienic to me.

In these days of disposable Bic razors it isn't so easy to get the old style loose blades anymore, and these can be difficult to use anyway, since incorrect handling can result in nasty cuts to the fingertips and hands which, as well as being inconvenient, is not the point of the exercise at all. The ideal solution to this is the common-or-garden craft knife; not one of those heavy duty, linoleum-cutter-cut-through-everything Stanley knives (after all, you're made of skin, not sheet metal), just a cheap, lightweight knife, available at any arts and craft shop for less than a pound, and usually sold with a few blades to spare. This is doubly practical since it is small enough to fit into a handbag or a pocket, while it is also easy to think of an excuse for carrying one: 'I was making a collage' or 'I was opening some letters'. Note: do not try the self defence excuse ('It's in case I get mugged') as this makes it an offensive weapon and you could get arrested.

The next issue is location and, frankly, there is only one answer to this; the bathroom. Even in shared accommodation you can always find an excuse for being in there a long time and, if you so wish, being naked (which prevents the staining of clothes). This makes any mess easy to clean up. There are some who insist on doing it in their bedrooms, or those die-hard exhibitionists who do it in the corner at other people's parties, but anyone who has ever tried to get bloodstains out of a carpet will know how unsatisfactory a solution this is.

Sexual Deviants – Extract

Ilse Danby

'How does he do it then?' I asked Emma, 'do you try to keep him away?'

'I'll come and show you.'

The others howled with glee while Emma climbed onto my bunk and lay on top of me. She kissed me, I struggled and thumped her with my fists. I screamed, 'Get off! Get off!' Her hands slid over my bare belly. I shivered, struggled less.

Suddenly, a blinding light. Gisela stood in the open door. Just like mother with her stern authority. She was one of the chosen. Tall, blond, knew the ideology back to front, our Camp Commander.

'Right, both of you, get into your track-suits and plimsolls.' Mine were stiff with cold and wet from this morning's run, the laces hard to pull.

'Come on, hurry up!'

She marched us into the shower. I lagged behind. She grabbed my left upper arm hard, dug her nails in.

'Get a move on,'

'Ouch' I yelled.

One cubicle each.

'Right, strip. Five minutes..'

She stood by and leant against the white tiled wall, one foot across the other, timing us. She looked profoundly bored. It was the middle of winter. Icicles hung from the roof. They glittered like steel blades in the naked shower light. I was not sure at first if the water was scalding or freezing. The shock stopped my breath. I shook from head to toe. The tip of Emma's nose was purple, her eyes red-rimmed.

'We do not tolerate any sexual deviants in the Third Reich,' Gisela said, 'you will be reported to Headquarters, both of you.'

'Will we be expelled?' I asked hopefully.

Gisela showed us to separate detention cells with barred windows, a sack of straw and a blanket on the floor. A month's latrine cleaning, daily, before breakfast.

I examined my arm. Four perfect half moons had appeared on the skin, still white amongst the reddened flesh. Mother had never warned me against women.

Re-Creation

Sylvia Forrest

It was the advert in the Echo
that first gave me the idea.
Taxidermy, it said.
Preserve Your Pet.
So, I had the canary stuffed
and then the cat.
The taxidermist did a real good job;
You wouldn't believe how lifelike they looked.

George, my husband said
"That fellow will be stuffing me next" .
I thought what a good idea
and not wanting to waste time
I killed him -
between the grapefruit and the cornflakes.
It stopped his moaning on.
George hasn't looked so serene for a long time.

But I miss the friction...
The taxidermist brings his brown case of implements.
Soon George looks his usual miserable self.
Tax makes a suggestion.
Would I like to be in an exhibition?
Me and George will be the star turns.
George scowling in his chair, and me
reaching forward to switch on the television.

Truth In Fiction

Sylvia Forrest

As the back end of a Panto horse
I marched with the Wrens
behind the Royal Marine Band.
Then, with beating heart, sang
Blow The Wind Southerly
into the Slovak night air, while
a shooting star dived down a Danish sky.
On the Champs Elysee,
I watched the Tour de France
after not knowing it was the day it was there.
On the strength of that
I made a spider head of my company;
tossed three piece suites like confetti
all along the Great North Road,
did a bungee jump from the
Empire State Building
and ended up
with one foot
in the North Sea
and one foot in the Baltic.
The sea weren't half rough.
Look, here's the photograph.

*Both poems published 'Waltzing Off from Hand-Me-Downs',
Diamond Twig, 1997*

Father's day

Sue Vickerman

Waiting in the porch for the organ, sweating already,
trying to scratch under my collar, then she's faffing
about with my damned cravatte. I tell her *walk steady*

and slap her hand picking at the silk roses on her fat
waist. Says she can't wait for her feet up with a fag
and the video later, after it's over, back at the flat.

We head off. Everyone's taking snaps, then that slag
she works with comes out in the aisle for a good view
and takes a full frontal. She's winking at the padre;

the fool smiles. The wife's gassing in the front pew,
the hat she bought for another wedding – daylight robbery
and they've split up already– but her jacket's brand new.

The padre on his Saturday job, can't be bad, making a bob
or two by dressing like a prat. We picked a good morning
for flowers, left from another wedding or a funeral; God
Almighty noticed my pocket. We kick off with that reading,
the one that goes *Love is*… Hell. Always the same reading.

Communion Steward

Sue Vickerman

She pulls it out by its neck
from the crock in the pantry.
There's the clank of enamel on flags
but no struggle. The body in plastic
still-born, kept in the dark,
drops into her wheely-basket
and is dragged through the village,

past the shop, down the snicket –
via dolorosa – to the back steps
of the chapel and into the vestry
and is laid out on the slab
for the final act: slice off
the green flecks, then slice
and slice.

Accustomed hands undertake to lay
the pieces on a gleaming platter
to be offered up for old times' sake –
the buns at a wake; a handshake of
condolence – and those who are still
living take the offered portion
habitually, supposing it to be

eternal life.

Home Safe

Pippa Little

Suddenly it's late, he's left behind,
his mother warned him:
friends all run home,
October sky dingy as a wet sheet,
lemon stains on the horizon
spangling the mousy Tyne,
grass torn, mud-smudged round goal.
Cold tastes blood sour in his mouth
when he hears them, the loose-limbed
always angry ones, huge as pylons
humming with their ugly joy:
paki bastard, paki bastard, paki, paki,
he is centre of their circle
only their teeth visible in the dusk,
sparks seem to jump from their spiky hair.

Once he dreamed his father was a tree,
broad, strong-backed: he clutches with both arms now,
starts to climb as their boots kick in, his knees
scraping the muscly bole, his tears
smearing the rough bark of his father's bearded neck.
He can leave them far behind,
shin up, up, up.
Embed like a tick inside
this rustling stronghold
where his lungs sing
he is come home,
safe.

Night a long time come now
he rouses to his father's calling
raw edge of panic unravelling his name
and he licks his tears
as his father finds him.
How stiffly he lies
in his father's trembling arms,
trying to be weightless.

Time Is

Pippa Little

What is time? he asks
I study his dappled eyes
trying to remember.

What is time? he asks again
he will ask and ask
until I answer him.

My mother told me
time is what's inside your body, child,
all your good things,
your skin with its own smell.
Time sings in you, your music.

What is time? he asks
with his sleep-walker's eyes:
I hold both his hands open like a book.

Time is now, I say,
just now.
You here,
and me. This star
crossing our path.

'Sleeping Beauty'

Liz Atkin

For fifty years she has lain unconscious
deep down beneath a nostril glimmer
of daylight in the old Village Hall
patiently awaiting the kiss of life.
Thousands of suitors have leant over
fumbling attempts to start her heart
with pumping and pummelling Methods.
One man from Sick Berth Reserve
still keeps her tongue as a memento
of too eagerly clearing her windpipe.

Balding but dressed in her Sunday best
her dislocated joints and loose right foot
lie blanketed on broken baize, undisturbed
for slings, splints and stretcher practice
for many years until they break in
through loosened lavatory glass
three blockish blunt boys
who yank her awake and there is no
First Aid for what is done when they
discover that Sleeping Beauty has no cunt.

Both poems first collection, 'Glee With a Blue Background'
Diamond Twig '98

Sad Giants

Liz Atkin

You can see them playing
in the park, cap badges the size
of car radiators as they thunder past
on a scribble of raised rail
astride engines 'Titan' and 'Flying Lad',
big blunt fingers tickling into
watchfine cabs between their knees
to give off whistling plumes of steam
or standing alone on Townmoor hill
aerials poking heaven
as their cockpit cradled minds
loop, swoop, soar and tailspin.

Each one remembers how
as a child he became a Giant
on certain Sundays of the year,
taken to those little Utopias
built in Home Counties gardens

where they could lean on roofs
and stride a street in one
and trains ran constantly
stopped only by sister's sandal,
and on hearing the hymning organ
they'd watch like cats
for a two by two congregation
which never ever appeared.

See their cars parked, small
and empty in the distance,
they rarely have a passenger
and when they do she is
as rigid and expressionless
as the inhabitants
of those childhood model villages.

Counting

Marlynn Rosario

Listening, I tried to learn their words for counting:
Ti, hni, thoug, lei, nga, heau, khuni, shi, kou, tahse.
Awkward my London mouth chewed sounds; they blocked my nose,
balanced on my tooth tip, stuck in the back of my throat;
the family trick of tubing my tongue, didn't help.

They weren't the blue of Grandma's *Suppoplejojair*!
exploding strong as the roar of a chinthe lion.
I couldn't savour them like *balachow, lethow*.
Flute and drum said father, the lilt of gong and cymbal,
mirror-practise, swallow, beat it to perfection.

Throwing the hop-scotch stone, jumping the turn of the rope,
proudly I rolled their chant to friends, who laughed them back:
Tee hee hee, ponglay, nah nah nee nah, hoho, coon-shit.
The sounds spat from their London mouths, stuck in my throat.
Teeth-tightened, listening, I couldn't make the words count.

Glasstales

Marlynn Rosario

I accepted all that,
Alice, the animals,
bewigged amphibeans,
smoking insects.

I swallowed it easily,
the growing and shrinking
and growing.

Never quite fitting,
standing keyless outside unopened doors,
in danger of drowning in tears,
wanting answers to the wrong questions,
I understood all that.

Now, running hard to keep still,
days twist in my hands like long necked flamingoes.
Sometimes, I am one stretched conciliatory smile,
faceless, suspended in air.

Silent Storms

Heather Young

I struggle not to slip on iced paths.
Snowflakes swirl around the streetlamp
like bees in a hive: the new moon
on bent knee promises more frost.
"Your turn to put the car away".

Garage door slams shut, shuddering;
back door next: all draughts excluded
by excluder-strips, excluding everything.
Lock turns against the storm, confining
central-heating closeness.

After cheese sandwiches, trifle, we sit
in stolid T.V. glare, appositional.
"Forecast's snow", you announce unnecessarily.
When sleet thrusts crusted panes you ask
"There! Didn't I tell you?"

The washer-dryer turns automatically:
a radiator simmers soap and softener smells
from your socks, my bra, to wear tomorrow.
And I still seethe with slights of yesterday,
unresolved and smouldering.

Oblivious, you squint outside, wiping steam
but snow blocks your view: you grunt
"It'll blow over by tomorrow …
it's far too cold to last".
"Yes…" I say.

You relish B.B.C. News, football scores,
commentating, not needing assent.
I contemplate past storms, past calms,
my reluctant submission to pattern.
Deja vu.

Industrious, I unravel wool,
wish I'd hired a video; knitting
your next-season's cricket sweater,
mentally chest-measuring
without touch.

Defense

Heather Young

Her knickers peep
from boxpleats, navy
as an inkblot. Lo-Lee-Ta. LO-LEE-TA.
"Little pain" her Mother named her.
Lolita. Sweet pain,
its wound open and red as a poppy.

She stalks more silently than
a sleeping dog, breath
panting in dreams. She stirs me with claws
pink from the paint I daubed; pale as veal.
Mouthing lollipops, gyrating hula-hoops
she cuddles a baby-doll.

Her grimaces are bare as a goldfish
trapped behind glass, sucking
sucking a kiss. (*Oprah would cloak*
her pre-pubescent charms in Laura Ashley prints.
Rantzen would rouse Nations to react.
It has all been done before.)

Now she sniffs my skin
its rawness skunking hot. She wriggles
under, loves me, relishes
volcanic blood. Compulsive as daisy-plucking
she never stops: never considers
I love her not.

Balaclava – Extract

John Barfoot

It began two days ago. I don't know about you, but I always have trouble with new shoes. I have to go through a breaking-in period to get my feet acclimatised. It's messy and quite painful, because what I do is walk barefoot in them for hours until my feet have knocked the leather into shape. By that time the shoes have been baptised in blood, and I must admit that I've rather ritualised this process on a sort of *through pain to enlightenment* basis. I take pride in not removing any grit or gravel that works its way in between me and the shoe, and have been known to actually add some myself if the process is proving disappointingly painless. I regard the dark brown stains that persist in the leather as a badge of honour. My brother calls me a *weird little fucker*, but I don't know - we're each of us weirder than we know, and wouldn't life be drab if we weren't? For instance, he regards the little wire cage around his balls as perfectly normal: *taming the old adam* he calls it as he tightens it a twist or two every morning, grunting as if he's lifting something really heavy. Weird or what?

Anyway, what happened was that I came back from my first ten-miler with these new shoes and when I eased them off, swabbed away most of the blood, and carefully rolled the broken skin back over the exposed flesh of the burst blister areas - I like that bit, especially the little liquid suck as the clear fluid that oozes out of the rubbed bits glues the flaps back down – I noticed that the ball joint at the side of my left big toe looked strange. The skin had been abraded rather more than usual, and it looked and felt as if the bone had been exposed. But what was visible – like a little dome erupting through the top of a small hill – was brown instead of white. I rubbed it a little and it felt rough. I rubbed some more, trying to clear the skin around it, and to my surprise, felt a sharp pain in my finger. I jerked my hand away and examined the finger closely. There was what looked like a splinter of wood in it – I could see its sharp point clearly under the skin, and the blunt end stuck up from my finger almost an eighth of an inch. I managed to get hold of it with my fingernails and work it free: it was definitely a wood splinter.

Extract

Joycelynn Grieves

I've been to the Museum today. I don't think as Museums go it's all that good, but I've always liked it. I used to go with mother when I was small, and it was so big and full of wonderful things, but everything always seems like that when you look back doesn't it ?

The Winter Gardens were the bit I liked the best, they were joined on to the back of the Museum but they got bombed in the war. They were another world to me, full of great big frondy plants, and it was all drippy and had a warm moisty smell about it. I remember there were black and white tiles on the floor, and puddles of water all over, and there was a round pond absolutely teeming with goldfish right in the middle. I remember sticking the toe of my shoe in it once, and if I close my eyes now I can still see that shoe in among those fish. The toe end was very round and it had a strap across the top and a button on the side. Mother always said afterwards when I used to talk about the pond that it was never like I thought, there were a few fish in among the lily pads, but that was all. Funny, because to me, looking back they were like millions of peach slices in a very big tin.

I liked the parrots in the cage in the corner, particularly Billy the oldest one, he was such lovely colours. His language was colourful as well, he would tell you to go to hell as soon as look at you, but there were no four letter words, not then, or at least if there were they didn't reach my ears.

Anyway, in the evening paper the other night there was an article on the Winter Gardens and Billy got a mention. Apparently they stuffed him when he died, and he's still there as large as life. I was a bit surprised because I've never seen him. The only stuffed thing I've ever seen is the lion that came with the travelling circus and mauled his trainer, who was lucky to leave the town alive. He came back five years later and caught typhoid, and this time, poor man, he wasn't so lucky, he died. Funny thing fate. To get back to my story. I went and asked at the desk about this parrot, and they told me he was packed up with a lot of stuff which couldn't be shown because they haven't got room, but they said if I went back at half past one he'd be waiting for me.

"No," I said, "it's just a whim, I used to come to see him when I was a kiddie, it doesn't matter."

"No," they said, "come back and we'll have him out."

Well, I'd been going to go straight home, but I decided to have lunch in town, and I went to British Home Stores. I had fish, chips and peas, a slice of bread and butter and a cup of tea for £1.80. I thought that was quite cheap, especially as I only needed a sandwich later for tea. It was really nice.

When I got back to the Museum they showed me into a little room, and left me on my own, and there he was, sitting on his perch, in the centre of the floor, my friend Billy !

He looked smaller than I remembered and a bit faded I thought, but it was him alright.

"Hello," I said, "remember me ?" I put my finger out and touched the top of his head, it was so nice to meet up with him again after all that time, then the door opened behind me and an old man came in. I recognised him straight away. He was the one I'd shared my table with at British Home Stores.

Purple Glossy Starlings – Extract

Celia Bryce

Binta's daughter is everywhere. She will not budge. From everything I do, or see. From everything I think or say. Each breath I take is stolen from her. She is everywhere and I cannot escape her.

And Binta herself. Measuring my every move. Her great heavy eyes, sliding down at me as she moves dust around with her cloth. Flicking at the pictures on the wall, at the door frames and the blinds. Once we laughed and talked together, in halting English, halting Mandinka. Once Binta danced with the drum-beater. Binta and her daughter. Dancing. Tall, sinewy. Beautiful, the two of them, and smiling. Always smiling. This is how I remember them. How I tell it to my mother in letters home. It is a simple thing to recall Binta dancing with her daughter. To describe the parties. The workers and their children dancing. It is easy to write about the colours and the smells; the meals Binta cooks; the fireflies in the evening. My words tell of how good it is here. A fiction my mother believes. Such is the beauty of living in a country she knows nothing about.

A month ago I might have sent Binta home, back to her village which is a mile from the compound, which is what should happen when a worker abuses her position. I came back from the clinic, one day, to find her in my bath. She had frothed up the water and sunk deep into it until only her head and her knees were visible. I watched from the doorway as she stood up and wiped the suds from her body, slowly as if waiting for each bubble to burst; scooping up a fistful and holding them up to the light; blowing them, like a child. Binta turned to face the window where the sun came through in slats and her face grew into a deep smile as she climbed over the side of the bath and into a bath sheet. My own bath sheet.

It is a sackable offence, taking a bath in the employer's house. There is a river to bathe in. I have seen her, proud and naked to the waist washing with the other women, sluicing down their daughters. They are like Glossy Starlings, the blue ones and the purple ones in the garden pond beneath the Flame-Tree. The people in the house before me told of Mourning and Nemaqua Doves in his pond, of Weavers and Red Bishops. Left photographs in frames. Told me to look out for them. I have seen only starlings. Purple Glossy. Blue Glossy. White Eyed. They are like Binta and her daughter. Sleek in the sun by the river.

But here she was in my bathroom, looking at me through the steam. The bath sheet was close around her shoulders and her eyes huge and wary. Crying. It wasn't a smile I had seen but something silent, like fire, pulling at the muscles of her face, pulling until her teeth were bared, as if every muscle and ligament in her face had contracted in the heat. I held out my housecoat. It only reached her knees.

'What is it, Binta?' She did not answer but shook her head, taking the sponge to clean out the bath. 'It's alright, just leave it,' I said. Binta continued scrubbing at the bath until I took the sponge from her hand. Her skin was ridged like bark. 'Tell me. Tell me about it.' Binta's long neck shone, her violet-black skin studded with globules of water.

'Look - I'm not going to sack you.' She stopped and faced me. Stared. Her chestnut eyes sunk deep in their yellow brown beds. 'Let's sit down,' I took her hand and led the way along the corridor to my bedroom.

Doorstepping – Extract

Jude Weeks

I was upstairs on the number sixty four deciding on beefburgers or mince for tea when I heard them talking. It's that Maggie from the pub, they whispered, and his poor wife doesn't know a thing about it, I had it from our Norma at the off licence, she hissed loudly, and she should know. Gossiping women with chins, and sad hats that my Nana would be ashamed of. I stood up. A heavy silence followed me all the way off the bus.

Next thing I knew, I was standing outside her house, still and thin as a shadow, watching them. They were together on the sofa and the curtains open. A silent film reeling on forever and ever. I could hear Mam's voice clearly, look at them, have they no shame, making a show of themselves for all the world to see. He had his arms around her and he was looking right into her face.

He glanced up and saw me, and smiled that way he did. It always used to win me over. lf he hadn't smiled I wouldn't have done it. I might have crawled away and hidden myself like a worm, but once he'd seen me there was nothing else to be done. She had a sad rock garden covered with weeds. The stones were painted white.

I love the sound of breaking glass.

She was out on the step within seconds, shouting at me, her mouth a big black square. Seemingly I was to blame for everything. All the neighbours came to their windows, no lace curtains to twitch on this street. Jenny Jackson flung hers wide open and hung out from her waist. When I looked up she waved at me, go for it, Hayley. She yelled. No pretence, but that's the way I like it.

Her name was Maggie. She waited on at the Red Lion, and you could hear her right down the street, and she hadn't altered much. He used to say can't stand a woman with a gob on her, but that was back then. He soon had a change of heart the minute she opened her legs, Mam said sourly, along with half the town. She's always had a big fan club.

Sitting with Mam in the park, watching the kids playing on the swings, running around without a care in the world. How long ago that time seemed to me. Mam buttoned up her cardy in a bad tempered way, jerking out her elbows. D'you know what it is about both of them, she said, she's a trollop and he's a fool, let them get on with it. She rustled in her bag and put a toffee in her mouth. But I expect you'll go your own way as usual. He was my man after all, she knew I wouldn't listen.

Maggie stood in her pink curlers and took the fag out her mouth just long enough to start calling me frigid as if she knew me or anything about me. Shouting for all the world to hear, give your man your hole once in a while and he wouldn't need me. With him standing there looking from her to me and back as if he couldn't make a decision on his own. I stared at him and there was nothing behind his eyes. Somewhere nearby, a dog barked.

A big black something was collecting inside me and it came out in a sudden spurt. I stepped forward and swiped the cigarette out of her mouth. Shock showed on her face. Hang on, he said, shaking me, never caring if I was hurt, you can't carry on like this. He was standing up for her, when it seemed only yesterday that nothing was more important than me and his bairns. I love you more than the whole world, he said then.

Candle

Margaret Perry

The night they held the folk-singing at Kinvarra
there was standing room only in the basement bar
when I slipped in beside a young American.

Together we sipped our stout, tapped a foot
to the jigging fiddles, and sang moodily
of how the swan in the evening moved over the lake.

And in between, we talked of mountains and music.
A guitar leaned against his chair and, yes,
he played, wrote songs, returned to the Burren

every Summer to walk the limestone endlessly
alone. No-one could match his stride, he said,
twisting a smile but his eyes were empty

bleak as trees on the stone-flagged hills, raked
by wind, their limbs spiked silver under a predatory
moon. If anyone lingers there he is changed

bewitched, like a seventh son with his second sight.
When the music stopped he ducked away under beams.
I never knew his name but still he haunts me.

He was a candle burning low.

The London Waiter

Margaret Perry
(for Max, who now lives in Dublin)

He moves between tables with the practised ease
of a heavyweight boxer, confident, light on his feet,
neat ears, a well set head on muscular shoulders.
His round eyes blaze above the broadest sweep
of white whiskers ever seen on a black face.

He is dynamic; but not your man for the swanky
bistro where late-night opera buffs loll about
nor the dapper chap who simpers through potted palms
at maiden aunts with their troupes of ballerinas;
though I can see they might find him very attractive.

He is more of an eel-pie stallholder or the lad-
about-town who slams down your mug of red hot coffee
beside a new baked bagel. You would not want to meet him
halfway home down a dark alley. And yet
I long for this furry ruffian to climb on my lap.

Note: 'The London Waiter' is a recognised breed of cat, a large longhaired black with white shirt-front, paws and whiskers.

27 Newhouse Road, Esh Winning

Maureen Almond

'And those who loved good music ceased to sing '
(Brendan Kennelly, 'My Dark Fathers')

There was no music in the house.
We were counted in by an iron snek
rapping on the gate.

And I've lost the tune of her voice
though not the orchestrated crack
of cinders in the grate

or the horse-hair crush
of the sofa, dark-greened on the back
wall. Brass rings tinkled

like triangles when I pushed
back the velvet drape in front of
the stairs. My feet, cymbals

clattering on the last three curved
lino steps, to land with a clap
on the coconut mat at the bottom.

Flames brushed a rhythm to the shiny
fender beat while spark
meteorites allegroed up the chimney.

At table, in her special place,
she maraca'd empty cotton reels –
strung them together for me, into a necklace

and stood a figure-eight of dominoes
to quaver patiently so I could tumble
them through a curving crescendo.

The dresser drawer creaked its
goodbyes when she reached for a bullet
for a good girl to eat on the bus home.
Her pats on Dad's shoulder were composed,
there were repeats not to leave it so long
next time. Kisses were pianissimo

but there was no music in the house.

I Know Exactly The Sort Of Woman I'd Like To Fall In Love With If I Were A Man.

Maureen Almond

She would flambé and bubble like Tina
Turn her temperature to more than fifty.
The rough wild husk of her voice would lift me
to way past boiling point. Oh this Prima
Donna of my fantasy, I've *seen* her
drooling at me. A hot chilli kiss she
blew, landed on my plate once, it missed me
by a spare rib - made my taste keener.

As for me, I'm already shimmering
in a thin glaze. I can turn up the heat
whenever I want to. I'm simmering
waiting to be whisked along with her beat.
She doesn't know, but in the glimmering
of her eye, I'd be good enough to eat.

(After Deryn Rees-Jones)

Soon – Extract

Sheila Mulhern

You know where she lives now.
And you genuflect. Mass started long since. You like kneeling when they're all standing. You like knowing where she lives.
You waited at the end of the lane, watching her, almost more than watching. You leant against the hot, blistery garage door facing her. It scorched your shoulder but you pinned yourself to it. Anyway she could hardly see the annoyance hammer at your face, the way it always does when something hurts you. Not from that distance.
"...My own fault, my own grievous fault," you intone mutating from sated peace to excitement. In between you go somewhere else. You swallow your pill. "Good boy," you say to yourself. Now you know where she lives. You had to say something to her. You lounged there, sweating and watched the litter of sneezy blossom and honesty flaring upright amongst the tins and flapping carrier bags as she drew on, closer and closer. But you couldn't speak. You were seeing your curly hair, your lumpy nose, your eyes that were sucked away with such venom your organs kaleidoscoped and you nearly choked. You smoothed your fringe with your smelly moist fingers. She was looming up over you and you couldn't think of anything and then the yard door banged shut and she was gone.
That was her.
They all go 'huu-um' and clear their throats and scrape their feet like their shoes are made of breeze blocks. You've combed your hair and you keep plastering it down with the flat of your hand and glancing back at the new people, a lovely family. After a while they stop smiling back at you, even the lady.
Mass peters out and you hang around thinking about what to do. The man from S.P.U.C. gives you a cheery red badge but Father Ignat isn't friends with them so you just hold it in your hand. When Father nips out for a fag, you slip into the vestry. Not two weeks ago, you nipped a cutting from his lemon geranium on the window ledge leaving just some woody thread, a damp hair dangling. Since then you've been watching it closely, seen it lushing up into a warped little tendril, pushing up from nothing, from a stump.
"Thomas!"

"Father Ignatius is this a weed, this nylon looking one?"
"No Thomas" he slips off his cassock and unwinds the rope from around his belly. He mutters a blessing at his strewn vestments, taking in your smeared shirt, watching you. He clears his throat. "Now I did ask you not to come in when I'm not here."
"It grows like something mad," you say.
Father Ignat dumps his fags down on the cluttered window sill and squints at the plant. Watery eyes glisten and you feel a vein pulse through him. "Isn't it a marvel?" he whispers.
"Like a little angel unfurling up to Heaven?" you say.
"Mmmh," says Ignat.
"Like a little rush of cancer?"
"Ah now Thomas," he's backing away from you, telling you it's a lovely day and you really shouldn't be coming in here when he's out.
"The rush in Mam's eye. It spurted out everywhere like a bursted river."
You splat your throat, your stomach. You should splat between your legs but not in front of the priest.
"Now Thomas we don't want to be going backwards again now do we."
"With her dead, I can go and trace my real mother, my birth mother."
"God save 's Mrs Finn was your mother," he snorts.
Sometimes you make him nervous, his bog accent kicks in when he's nervous. "We're all looking for our parents even those reared on top of them. Now let's have no more of this tracing nonsense. Birth mothers!"
He's pulling on a nun-knitted sweater muttering on about privacy.
You look at the mess on the windowsill and Ignat looks at you. "Mrs Finn, God rest her, raised you like one of her own, she was more a mother to you than some slip who abandoned you twenty years ago."
You're not listening to him. "Like Father? Like what? She couldn't have children. She didn't have a W.O.M.B."
He's buck upright, he might floor you with his curling fat fists and you don't care. She didn't have a W.O.M.B. She wasn't supposed to have children. It wasn't meant. The person who was meant to have you is your birth mother, the words thrill you. She is very close to you now and you know where she lives.
Fr. Ignat's breathing has calmed a bit. "God gives us all challenges," he sputters. "Now take your flukin tablets!"
Frowning at his language, you wander outside. It's blinding, the sudden, dry light of the graveyard and you blink your weak eyes against it.

Trade

Trisha Jones

We journeyed for three days
to the camp of the Nambikwara.

Our guides and mules wove ways
across the untracked terrain

and all we could do was trust
in our saddle-packs and promises

to appease any blood lust.
We joined the squaws, papooses

late on the second afternoon
and slept better that night.

We rode into the camp at sundown
of the third day, by a waterhole

at the foot of the sacred mountain.
No scalps swung from a totem-pole

and the meat that cooked on fires
had the look and smell of venison.

We ate as they did, from fingers,
licked at the juice that dribbled

from knuckle to wrist. By moon
and firelight, I scribbled

some notes in my journal.
They circled my stool

to watch me write,
like children new to school.

They drilled me with eyes
that had never seen whites

or imagined our ways;
did not know what to do

with the pencils and paper
we gave, preferred the steel

of our knives. And yet later
we saw them trying to write,

clenching at pencils in the way
they might wield their machetes.

Lines wavered and snaked grey
across the pages of grubby white,

and said nothing that they couldn't
already interpret, in the height

of the gathering clouds, the hint
of footprints in the dust.

Wise to a touch of wind, a scent
of air, a tremble of the ground,

they lived by signs that meant
nothing to our muffled senses.

We counted their numbers: divided
by gender, multiplied for summers

and subtracted long winters, decided
to take the final figures

and round to the nearest ten.
They could not count, yet none

would overlook a missing horse
or child, all knew how much

deer would feed their visitors,
wood could fuel the night fire.

For five days we ate their meat,
drank their water, breathed their air.

On the sixth, we prepared to leave;
the sky promised good riding weather.

We had a little Nambikwaran, tongues
circling new words, trading farewells.

Women Are Like Fruit

Trisha Jones

He likes his bananas sleepy,
the taste of bruised peach;
peels oranges with his teeth.

She prefers root vegetables,
the way they grow in the dark,
the excuse of onions.

His teeth are white and strong,
bite through the skin of an apple,
wince at the taste.

Her mouth is spitting seeds,
she sweeps them up,
strings a necklace.

When the necklace is full,
she will leave.

Michael's Mother Tells A Story

Jane Wood

It has snowed in the night. You fetch the boots your father bought last weekend when you stayed with him. But then your mother says you don't have to go to school. She says you have a cough. So you put the boots away. And stay indoors all day with her. With the gas fire on. And the silence of snow at the window. You eat what you can find. Beans and eggs. The crusts of an old loaf. Soup. You don't even go in the yard because she doesn't want to break the white crust that spreads from kitchen door to gate. After the soup your mother tells a story. The story of Cumbard. A strange green light from the snow fills the room. As your mother becomes Cumbard. Wearing him as a shawl round her shoulders.

A child was ill. The people clamoured. Send him to Zelt, they said, Zelt has the magic. But the child was too ill. Zelt must come to us, I told them. Gather the berries, I said, prepare the pulps. We must do what we can.

A message came. Zelt was entertaining a knight who searched for the Holy Grail. We had to understand that he could not walk out on such a man. He would come when he could.

The child died. And then Zelt came.

He came like a snake sliding amongst us. With his supple body that suggested the rhythm of a dance. With his subtle words that seemed a song, though we could not be sure a song was there. We strained our eyes to see the dance. We strained our ears to hear the song. Then we began to see, began to hear. We had the idea of something like a bird - the softness of its breast, the strength of its wings. We glimpsed the glory of its flight.

Look upwards, Zelt told us. To the stars and beyond.

Look outwards. Past the horizon.

Zelt sent out expeditions. He evoked spirits. He danced. He sang. He dipped into this, then that. Then lost interest. He slept for a week. The people were at a loss. Till the fields, I told them. Tend the sheep.

But they were made for better things than that. They looked outwards now toward golden kingdoms. They look upwards toward silver stars. Honour was no longer a question of mending fences. They laughed at my slowness of mind in not comprehending this. They spat as they passed, blaming me for the child.

I found Zelt resting in the gully beneath the ledge of overhanging rock. A woman was painting his body. The crops were ruined. It was time for the sheep to come down from the hills. The people did nothing but bicker.

He had been waiting for me. I saw it in his eyes. But there was something else. Something that fluttered. Something that would not stand still for me to understand it. And then it was gone. And only a nakedness was left to his eyes.

He tried to move. But I had hold of him. I am a big man. A strong man. I lifted him above my head. His lithe body. I thumped it down on the ledge of stone. His poetry. His supple dances. His large and wonderful ideas. I smashed them on the rock. I smashed dark skinned, snake-like Zelt. His skull.

No-one spits at me now. And no-one laughs. The sheep are tended. The crops grow. The seasons turn.

Your mother takes the shawl from her shoulders. She sits down amongst the cushions. The room has become dark. It is lit only by the fire. But she will not turn on the light. Not yet. Not until she has asked her questions. You can feel them looming.
Who do you like best?
Best of who?
Zelt or Cumbard? Who do you believe in?
I like them both.
But which best?
I don't know.
Which is like your father?
Neither.
If you could save one of them which one would it be?
Cumbard.
Why?
I'd save them both.
You can't.

Then Cumbard.
Why?
He's safer.
Safer isn't always best.
She puts you to bed. She bends to kiss you. In the dark, which is never quite safe, in the place between waking and sleep, Zelt slides in. What was that look in his eye?
Was it sad and beautiful – you close your eyes to see – like the look in Mum's eyes when she spoke of him?

Wimberry Pies – Extract

Helen Astley

I took books up to the den - old Rupert annuals from Grandma's sideboard drawer. Stephen loved the pictures and I used to read the stories to him.

Once in the middle of a story, Stephen suddenly clamped his hand over my mouth. His eyes were large. '*Shh!*' he hissed loudly. There was a clopping sound in the lane behind us and an 'Eh up!' While Stephen sat frozen I stood up and poked my head through a gap in the roof. There were little orange blobs of fungus round the edge and pale dust sprinkled onto my sleeve. In the lane was Mr Swithenbanks with his dog. He looked at me and then turned away and clopped on.

Sometimes Stephen brought a wimberry pie his mother had made. We sat in the corner on the straw, breaking pieces off the pie and eating them, holding our necks out so that the juice would not stain our clothes. Then we went home with purple fingers.

Auntie Eileen said it wasn't right to keep asking Stephen's mother to make pies. I never had asked, but one day I spent nearly two weeks' pocket money on a wimberry pie from the shop. The lady took it from the sloping shelves in the window and put it into a paper bag. She frowned and just as I dropped the sneck to close the door I heard her start to say, 'If that were my child…'

We took the pie up to the den and sat inside where it was cool. Our backs were against the mossy wall and sunlight coming through a hole in the roof made stripes across our legs. The sky was blue. Outside our little den the grass sighed.

We sat with the pie between us. As I lifted it from its clean white bag and broke off the first piece, Stephen suddenly made a high pitched *warbling* sound. I couldn't tell what he was trying to say. Sometimes I could; sometimes I couldn't. He bent over my legs and I watched as he scooped up a small green beetle. He held it gently in his hand, coming close to me for a moment so that I could see. Then he crawled to the doorway to set it free. His short legs flailed behind him. A foot struck the piece of pie, squashing it against my legs.

Poor Stephen let out another cry when he saw what he had done. Wimberry juice splattered over my skirt like drops of blood. I pulled it round to see the stain spreading over the cream material and knew I couldn't go back to Grandma's like that. But we were playing house. I would have a washing day. There had been rain in the night and the lane was full of puddles. I stood up and began pulling down the skirt.

'No, no!' cried Stephen. 'Swinbacks!' He pointed to my bare legs and white knickers. 'Swinbacks!' he said again. He was anxious in case Mr. Swithenbanks should come down the lane and catch me, undressed. I couldn't go outside the den in my knickers.

So Stephen took my skirt. He folded it carefully and went out into the lane to look for a good puddle. I watched from inside while he dipped it and rubbed it and spread it on the wall. Then we sat in the den waiting for it to dry and every few minutes Stephen looked out, ready to whisk it away if Mr. Swithenbanks and his dog appeared.

Mobile – Extract

Ellen Phethean

The trouble with Stacy is she won't take her tablets – then she's up, she's down. Running round the house, making the dog howl. Well, it's obvious she can't come back here. I tell the Prison Social Woman:-
"She can't come here. She'll upset everything."
"But Brenda," she says, they're very forward like that, "it's in Stacy's best interests."
"My name is Mrs Hardcastle," I say, "And there's another thing. She's changed, being inside." I just switch the phone off. We aren't getting anywhere and I've got a friend due any minute. I look out of the window, for Charlie. It's hard to see anything much through the wire mesh. There's Iceland on the corner, and Singh's - where I get my pop and paper. They know me, it's waiting when I arrive. They call me Mrs Hardcastle. "How are you today ?" they ask. So polite.
And Arthur's another problem, with his smile and wavy hair. Arthur is much too interested. He's just a big problem is Arthur.
He remembers Stacy when she was ten and used to call him Uncle. She's changed. Older. Loopy. No knowing what she'd say. To anybody.

I tap the phone. It's a mobile. Sometimes I think it may be accidentally on, listening to me as I talk. I say hello sometimes - to see if anyone'll reply. They spy on you, these Social people. I never visited Stacy. I can't bear the smell of Elastoplast and cooked dinners. They all smell like that: hospitals, schools, prisons. Round here they all look the same too. That's what Stacy's Auntie Susan said, that's why she got out. She was on a package holiday in the Algarve and won a Karaoke contest in Portimao. Got spotted by a talent scout. Now she's on Portuguese TV - she's the one who presses the button to start the Lottery Balls. The Lottery's big in Portugal. Susan won't come back:
"What ? To grey skies and padlocks ?" she says.
Susan's got a lemon tree in her yard. She's made something of herself. Stace'll never make anything of herself, except an exhibition. I said to the Prison woman:
"Prison's the best place for Stacy if she can't be trusted. I've got my own life to lead." Charlie agrees with me, "Brenda" he says, "Think of yourself."

Charlie's a builder. Got a crinkly face and brown arms. Body like a JCB, all hard from lifting scaffolding. He won't take no for an answer, will Charlie - like a bulldozer. Gets what he wants - I'm putty in his hands. He knows it too. I like a man who makes things happen. He says:
"Brenda - you got to be ruthless. "
I say: " No tiles, that's me. Roofless" And when I laugh, he grabs me. He can't resist me when I laugh. Not like Arthur.

Charlie's late. He's usually here by now, that's the arrangement. I'll see his blue Ford pickup parking in the back lane, he hoots and screeches the breaks. Charlie's that sort of man.
There's my mobile ringing - if it's that prison woman again, I'll tell her straight, No.
"Hello ? Oh, Charlie - where are you ? the Dog and Duck ? But I thought . .What are you doing there ? No, I'm not prying. No. Tomorrow'll be fine, whatever suits. OK What ? Stacy ? No. No! I'll tell her. Promise."
Oh, he's gone. He usually kisses the mouthpiece. And he likes to hear Mimi bark goodbye. "Mimi sweetie pie, my little doggy," - I love Jack Russells - "daft, aren't you tuppence ?" She hops in and out the cat flap.
"Never mind Mimi, we'll see Charlie tomorrow. Maybe one of the others will call. They bring you dog treats and nice surprises for mummy, don't they ? Sit ! There's a girl."

Divorce 1945

Joan Johnston

1

As I open the door the first thing
is the sun on the side of the desk,
last polished the day you got back
from the south of England –
mother had insisted, using a rag
and cream, from a tin. Then
your face, and from your shoulder
the metal glint of a wing.
Behind the door in my peep-toe shoes
I try to hear you breathe. Sometimes
I believe you are the quietest man
I've ever known.

2

Put me in a picture I said.
Just me somewhere on my own
where I can't disappear.
On a beach, my hair blowing hard
against a clear sky. And take me staring
straight at the camera.
A smile doesn't matter.
Just get me all in.

You

Joan Johnston

It's the way you look. You look
and make me take four beats
to a breath. Step on a line. Step
on a crack.

Last night I traced the edge
of a pattern on the sheet
without moving, while you still stirred
downstairs. And I recognised Florida
and a dog's head where
the plaster has fallen
It's all because of the way
you look.

I have a thumbnail
that fits beneath three other nails
perfectly, while at the same time
there's a rhyme that I work
against my teeth with my silent tongue
all day. Because of the way you look
I am making an atlas
of the world in my room.

Both poems published first collection
'What You Want' Diamond Twig '98

Waiting for Mary

Lisa Matthews

Grace in the sail-loft
watches as people
walk along the seafront.

She opens the window to taste
the salt, the wet sheet light
falling across her shoulder,
down her arm
where it lies in a pool
in her opening hand.

The brandy smells rough
and takes her away to when

they visited London,
her, Mary and mother and father.

Then somebody bursts a balloon.
It's been a long time for the band
and the hands that hold cornets and
scorn children to be still.
Tipping sand from shoes,
it's never ending.

The landlady flicks some ash
on the doorstep and casts an eye
up the long dark stairs.
She's going to tell
them tonight,
those two.

Walking with horses

Lisa Matthews

I've been awaited like rain
and ignored like a symptom
but now I see fields
in every direction.
These fields are not of
wheat, blood or tears,
no – they just seem
empty
impassible to me.

It's eight o' clock.
The shadow of a man
with a spade
crosses the muddy path,
then I see you in the distance
walking with horses.

The Day Lenny Nearly Died

Bob Cooper

It's six in the evening, the streetlights coming on,
though the Cathedral clock struck three minutes ago,
and I've already been to The City Vaults,
had a Tetley's, bought 20 Silk Cut,
then glanced in at the Blackie Boy,
where Tommy behind the bar said he hadn't seen you,
and there was Lenny near The Imperial,
pissed as usual, lighting a roll-up and trying to sing,
but he didn't see me so that was O.K.

while the Marxism Today guy crossed over again –
the old one with the pony-tail and tartan D.M.'s
who I'd tried to ignore outside The Beehive
until he mentioned oppression and I'd got onto Stalin,
though he hadn't heard of Akhmatova or Mandelstam,
and he'd interrupted, said poetry was *unproductive,*
but, still in full flow, I'd switched to the Prague Spring,
flowers in the gun-barrels of tanks, then Jan Palach –
while Lenny sang on, *to brighten up even your darkest night* –
and I was reading Baudelaire when I'd heard of him,
Les Fleurs Du Mal for the first time, and a woman's hair
as rich as tobacco that I'd loved to have smoked, inhaled –
and now hearing again that hard-left tone as Lenny relights his tab,
holds his bottle like a microphone and continues to croon,
You just call out my name … while the finger-wagging starts
and he shouts over to me as the shoving begins

when this police car pulls up and they get out,
put on their caps, then stand each side of Lenny –
and I'm sure they're going to lift him – but this Socialist guy
gets hold of Lenny's Safeway Cognac, steps to one side,
turns his back, stuffs a hanky in the top,
tips it, lights it – though no-one else notices –
then throws it at the car, and it doesn't explode
until Lenny falls over – or is he pushed –

then everything flares purple blossoming light

and I see you over the road, running to them,
wrapping your coat round Lenny's hair,
shouting something so loud at the night
and our faces, like the Vltava, frozen over.

Marlowe

Yes, I do, I know that face: smiling, coming out of Dolcis in Eldon Square,
a dancing girl and Bali printed on his T-Shirt, and Kickers under his coat.
This is the child who the Head said during break was a bad 'un, who hadn't a clue,
who was always half-asleep: *no video, y'see, watches old films through the night*.
But that was last year when I'd filled in for Debbie and he'd unexpectedly said:
the Hoover in the corner looks like the cormorant I saw on a post in the Tyne.
Then I'd marvelled at that and said, *Yes, I can see what you see. Thank you*.

So I follow him up to the fountain – and how do you get hold of *A Pair* of shoes? –
and remember I'd quoted T.S. Eliot, who, when he'd lifted a phrase from Stravinsky,
said: *a good poet steals*. Then he'd grinned up at me again, wrote that down.
And he's joined by his smaller sister who shows off her new Pods while he tries his on
but she frowns, says something, and he agrees then drops them into a bin.

And can I go over and talk to him now as they wander across to Ravel,
where, like Bogart in The Big Sleep, he scratches his ear while he thinks
then talks to himself like someone who knows what he sees?

Fetish – Extract

Peter Straughan

1

The night before they sacked him, Ed dreamt he was a Lump-fish. He was an amazing thing of phosphorescence and transparency, hunted through deep night waters by Japanese fishermen. He looked it up in the Dream Book over breakfast. There was only an entry for 'fish' in general "New Beginnings" said the book. A Journey from One Life to Another." At work they gave him his wages for the month, minus the missing money. There was, they explained, no question of a reference. Ed nodded, wisely.

That night, brushing his teeth, he thought again of his dream. New Beginnings. He rose from the green swill of the washbasin and gazed at his reflection in the mirror, with great, blinking, fish-bulb eyes.

2

The night after they sacked him, Ed went for a walk. He cut a slow circle through the city, curving past the dark windows and down steep stairs to the river. At a corner he struggled to light his last cigarette. The wind rose behind him. Trees in the park cracked and groaned. Looking for a sheltered spot he found he was standing beside the deep, marble doorway of an old tenement building. He stepped into the darkness and lit his match. He was about to light his cigarette when he realised he was standing on someone's foot. He stepped into the wind, dropping the match. Maybe he even apologised. There was no reply. He stepped back into the doorway and, lighting another match, knelt and examined what it was he had stood on.

It wasn't a foot. It was a shoe, one of two women's shoes. The tall, curving heels were together, the toes slightly apart. Ed stared into the black liquid surface of the toes and caught his own reflection, tiny and trapped beside a pinpoint of flame. A word appeared in his mind. "Sphinx," said Ed, liking the word. "Sphinx."

3

In the morning, after toast, Ed examined the shoes on the kitchen table.

He made notes:
Right Shoe
Length – 25.5 cm
Width at widest point – 9.5 cm
Width at narrowest point – 4.5 cm
Height at heel – 12 cm
Height at toe – 3 cm
Angle of descent (heel to toe) – 25 degrees

Left Shoe
Length – 25 cm
Width at widest point – 9.3 cm
Width at narrowest point – 4 cm
Height at heel – 12 cm
Height at toe – 3 cm
Angle of descent (heel to toe) – 25 degrees

Odour: None. Suggests shoes barely worn. (Or woman barely sweats.)

Size: Large (Approx size nine). Suggests either a short to medium size woman with big feet OR a tall woman with feet in perfect proportion to her overall height.

Other: 25 degree angle of heel descent matched by original 25 degree angle of divergence between toes, when shoes were found.

Ed sat and read his notes.
"I am uncovering something here," he said out loud. "I am uncovering something marvellous here,"

4
It was only on the third day after they had sacked him that Ed changed the position of the shoes. He did it suddenly, as if inspired, pulling the toes together so that the shoes opened out into a V shape. This changed everything. Before the shoes had been cold, distanced, maybe even intimidating. Now they were sulking, a little spoilt, a little shy. He began to experiment with different positions of relationship between the shoes.

Smile Please – Extract

Chrissie Glazebrook

Tramp grabs me with his clammy paw. It's the last day of school, a non-uniform day. I'm in my cropped vest and flares from Top Shop and he's goggling at my belly button.
'Ah, Rowena'. His dandruff dances as he shakes my hand.
'You have gained a rare distinction: the only girl in your year to leave us unburdened by a single GCSE'. He's full of crap like this.
'And what brilliant career awaits, I wonder.'
'I wannabe a beautician. My dream job.'
'A beautician!' He blasts me with baccy and stale chewy.
'My best advice', he confides, like I'm interested, 'is to seek employment where smiling is not in the job description. You have a natural inclination to scowl.'
Right. I wriggle out of his sweaty mitt, head for the door. Freedom.
'Try shelf-stacking', he hollers after me. 'And remember the school motto: Live Worthily.'
Fat chance. I go down the Mall and rob two lippies and an eyeliner from Boots, stash them with the rest of the stuff in a sports bag at the back of the wardrobe. Its so full I can hardly zip it up.

Mum's on holiday from the chip factory. She takes me to the coast for a couple of days as a treat and we stay in this naff B&B with plastic flowers in hanging baskets. We parade up and down the front scoffing food from polystyrene trays and Mum twirls a chip in her fingers like it's a fancy cigar. 'Maris Piper,' she says and sniffs it. ' Yecch, the fat's tainted.'
She wants me to have a go at pitch 'n putt but I say I'd rather slit my veins so we go to Spanish City and play the bandits and pinballs and Mum wins a bread bin on the bingo. I'm wearing full make-up on top of Factor 15 but the sun still catches me and I look like a HobNob except for the two white frown lines on my forehead.
'You're on holiday. Stop clarting your face up, let your skin breathe', moans Mum. Puh-leeze. I'd rather stick pins in my eyes than go without make-up.
When we get home there's a letter asking me to call and see the Assistant Careers Adviser, Miss Pegram. I'm expecting some old wife with a perm but Miss P turns out to be a bit of a Goth. Her face is pure self-raising

with two black grapes for eyes and I recognise her lipstick, Plum Loco. She goes through the claims procedure. What a joke. I'm not entitled to a bean. She asks what sort of job I'm after so I feed her the old trousers about being a beautician or failing that, I say, I'd like to be in the movies. Her mouth puckers up all tight like a cat's bum. She says I have to be realistic and shoves a stack of leaflets on youth training programmes at me. I bin them on the way out.

Mum's cool about me not working. We have this routine: I lie in bed listening to my Discman till the pillows feel like rocks then I get up just before she leaves for the afternoon shift.

I go down the Mall. Word must be out, the orange-faced slappers in Boots watch me like hawks so I head down to Superdrug for some make-up. I've just palmed a Cafe au Lait duotone blusher with sable applicator when I see this lanky lad with glasses staring at me. He smells weird. I goes, 'You got a problem?' He doesn't look like a store dick but you can never tell.

'No, but you have.' He nods towards a mumsy woman down the feminine hygiene aisle. She looks away real quick and pops a box of tampons in her basket. I plonk the blusher back on the shelf and wander out dead casual. He's waiting for me. 'Cheers', I say.

'Fancy having a look round Hitz?' he says.

Maison wella. It's shoplifters heaven.

He's all arms and legs and nerdy-chic like Jarvis Cocker. His name's Dean and he lives on the Woodlea estate or so he says, its vee posh up there.

'Where you from?' he says.

'Scotswell.'

'I know it. Bandit country.'

He picks up a Charlatans CD and I'm covering him, waiting for him to slip it into his jacket, but he goes right up to the till and pays for it. Cash.

'See you then', he says when we're outside.

'Where you off to?'

'Back to work. Its my dinner hour.'

'Right. Later, yeah?'

'Later.'

The Vampire

Amanda Thomson

The Vampire
has her good days
and her bad days.
Today she is a
wisp
of a thing
with bluey-tinged
skin
like tissue-paper.
Sitting in her
wheel-chair,
waiting…
to die,
and for his letters.
He sends her
pictures of Dracule
and his news,
and sachets of his
blood,
and sometimes
a pair of false
fangs
that he has carved
and polished
himself.
She pops them in
and runs her tongue
over them.
The old days
pass across her face.
Though she cannot
walk and the
only place she goes
is the corner shop
with her mum,
in her head she
dances and flies
and wraps her
limbs around
strange blood-thirsty
creatures.
She orders expensive
clothes from
catalogues and
sits by the
window wearing them,
watching 'Countdown'

and writing to him.
He and she were
once upon a time…
They never had an
ending
He made her feel alive,
She made him feel
immortal.
They come from
the same town.
She stamps her
envelopes with
bats and moons.
He keeps their
photographs
in the loft.
In some of them
she is a bat
clinging to his
thigh.
In the rest they are
placing things inside
of each other,
strings of pearls,
and rose-buds
and knives.
Angels of death,
twins,
still-lifes.
Pools of scarlet
around their feet.
He wears her
scars on his neck
wherever he goes
She waits also for
his return,
when he is done
with life,
when his name is
up in lights
and all the girls think
he is a creep.
She lapses sometimes
and has to have extra
blood pumped into
her professionally.
He always rushes to
her side,
crying all
along the
motorway.

Biographies

Liz Atkin trained as a visual artist at St Martin's School of Art, London, in the 70's. She had exhibitions in Europe and the U.K. including one at the Laing, Newcastle in '91. Two years ago she succumbed to a long-held desire to write poetry and she is now being published in various magazines, ranging from Chapman, Envoi, Staple, Smiths Knoll and Prop. She recently had her first collection published **Glee with a Blue Background**, Diamond Twig 1998.

Ilse Danby was born in the province of Mecklenburg, North Germany. She had to abandon her studies because of the circumstances of war and eventually fled to West Germany where, to survive, she obtained a translator's and bilingual secretarial post. She's now having some success with her stories and poems, after taking writing courses and joining writing groups.

Pauline Plummer is a North Eastern poet who has been widely published and broadcast, nationally on Radio 4, and in the region. Her collection **Romeo's Cafe** was published by Paranoia Press in 1992, and she has won various literary prizes: Tees Valley Writer National Competition and the Cleveland Literary Festival Competition.

Helen Astley has been playing at writing for most of her life. Now that she is nearly grown-up she is working for an MA in Creative Writing at the University of Northumbria.

Vera Kulkarni started with a poem in her school magazine. She never looked back. She is a prime mover behind the Write Together project, that runs workshops in South Tyneside, and she runs Seafield Publishing. Vera has had her work published in The Page, Hybrid, The Crack, her book **Women and Children First** was published by Seafield.

Pippa Little is a co-editor of Writing Women. She has a doctorate in Women's Poetry and won a Gregory Award. She is an adult education teacher in Newcastle upon Tyne. Her poems have appeared in many magazines and several anthologies.

Jude Weeks was born in North Shields and now lives in Gateshead. She has had several stories published and broadcast. She works in Newcastle as a counsellor.

Trisha Jones has written prose ever since she could spell and began writing poetry six years ago when she joined the Hexham Women's Writing Group. She has an uncompleted novel and is currently working on several essays.

Pat Stevens lives in Newcastle. She has three children, teaches part-time and is doing the MA in Creative Writing at Northumberland University. She is currently working on a collection of short stories.

Sue Vickerman was born in a semi in Bradford, working class credentials otherwise flimsy. After teaching-training, fled to eastern China, fell in love with a German. Sent articles home, had a couple of features in the Guardian. Finally came to Weardale with partner and they're currently living a staid life as lesbian Methodists in a country cottage.

Betty Weiner was born in Vienna and came to live in England with her family as a refugee when she was three. Brought up in Wales, she's lived in the North East for the last 30 years. She has been attending writing classes since she retired 4 years ago. She won 3rd prize in Sunderland University's Northern Writers poetry competition and was commended for her Sid Chaplin Short Story. She is currently working on some short plays.

John Barfoot has been writing stories for as long as he can remember. Some of them have been published.

Bob Cooper has been published in numerous magazines and won many competitions, including the '93 Poetry Business, '95 Tears in The Fence and '97 Redbeck Press Pamphlet Competitions . Most recently he has been a winner in the PHRAZ '97 Poetry Competition and won the '97 Dulwich Festival Competition. He has a collection **Drinking Up Time**.

Ally May lives in Arthurs Hill, Newcastle upon Tyne. Loves to write poetry.

Peter Straughan was born in Gateshead in 1968. His stage plays have been produced in Britain and the US including 'Bastardhead', 'Heart of Darkness', '1812' and 'Rat'. He won this year's Alfred Bradley Award.

Maureen Almond is a retired personnel manager. She has been writing for four years and had her first collection **Hot** published in 1997 by Mudfog Press. She won the National Association of Writer's Groups Award for Best Free Verse in 1996 and was a runner up in the Capricorn International Competition.

Joycelyn Grieves has written and read three short stories for Radio Newcastle and had short stories published, all a number of years ago. She has recently returned to writing, and has been attending Writing From The Inside Out at Newcastle University.

Margaret Perry was born in cockney East London, but grew up in Kent, where she attended schools in shelters during the war. She married in her early twenties and spent 21 years as a clinical medical secretary in the NHS. Early retirement led to a concentration on writing and she has an anthology published by Mudfog Press, **Holy Ground**.

Ellen Phethean is a poet, who works with The Poetry Virgins. She has had three collections containing her poetry published, **Modern Goddess, Sauce** and **Modern Riddles**, and had a long radio poem broadcast on Stanza, BBC Radio Four.

Philippa Collingwood hates writing biographies but has a thing about peanuts and bananas. She was a late starter and has been published in among others, Iron. She has been a Peterloo prizewinner and has a poem going up on the Metro.

Ivy Hudson is married with two grown-up sons and works as a part-time library assistant for Durham University. She has been writing poetry for 17 years for children and adults, the latter mostly concerned with domesticity.

Liz King moved back to her native North East after 20 years away in the RAF where she was a medical scientist specialising in post mortems on aircrash victims. Since leaving she's worked at various medical establishments and is currently in the haematology department at the Royal Hospital, Sunderland.

Tracey Sinclair is a researcher from Newcastle, although she has spent much of her adult life in Glasgow, where many of her stories are set. Her work has been published in The Printer's Devil, Sky and Cutting Teeth, and she has been a winner in the Avenue short story competition and is included in this year's Arc Short Stories Anthology.

Jadwiga Billewicz designs and makes jewellery for a living. Recent years have brought a refocussing on her own writing and she is currently working on poetry, short stories and the initial stages of a novel. Her poetry has appeared in The Rialto, Smith's Knoll, Blade and Sending Messages, a local anthology edited by Linda France and Sean O'Brien. She has also received financial assistance from Northern Arts.

Joan Johnston lives near Newcastle. She has had poems published in Rialto, Smith's Knoll, Wide Skirt and Writing Women and has a pamphlet **Breathing In** published by Flarestack. Despite having two sons, a dog, an allotment and a husband she still manages to keep a canny cupboard. She has a collection **What You Want**, Diamond Twig 1998.

Kathleen Kenny lives and writes in Newcastle. She has been writing since the late 80's and has had numerous poems published over the last few years in magazines such as The Echo Room, Krax and Foolscap. She had a poem selected by Diamond Twig Press for their Amnesty International Postcard competition.

Lisa Matthews is 32 and works part-time for Mslexia. Primarily a poet, she is currently completing her first novel, for which she received a Northern Arts Writers Award.

Andrea Badenoch's first crime thriller **Mortal** (MacMillan 1998) was described as an impressive debut. Her second book **Driven** appears in August.

Celia Bryce lives in Tynemouth. She runs workshops for people with limited access to writing opportunities – prisoners and people with psychiatric problems. She gets much of her own material from working in bands. She's a singer and plays accordion and saxaphone, and writes songs and music for line dancing.

Sylvia Forrest was born in South Shields in 1932. She went into service at 14, and then worked for the ministry at Longbenton. A stint in a florist's eventually led to further education and poetry. She has a collection **Waltzing off from Hand-Me-Down**, Diamond Twig 1997.

Celia McCulloch is American born but has lived in the West End of Newcastle for seventeen years and often writes about that part of the world. She is now semi-retired and spends more time writing, gardening and making warm and colourful things out of fabric. Celia also advises a group of housebound writers, as part of Gateshead Library's Prime Time programme.

Chrissie Glazebrook has worked in a zoo, a vegetarian restaurant and in television and radio. Her articles have appeared in numerous magazines from Everywoman to Jackie. She is co-author of **The Pocket Guide to Men**. Her poetry has appeared in The Crack and in Writing Women and Smile Please, her first published short story, appeared in The Devil.

June Portlock lives in Gateshead. She read avidly as a girl and a neighbour assured her mother she would develop a brain tumour as a result. She has had her work published in a number of magazines and anthologies – Tees Valley Writer, New Fiction and the Poetry Virgin's collection **Sauce**. She has also won and been runner up in numerous competitions, including Sid Chaplin. She has a collection **Broken Biscuits**, Diamond Twig 1997.

Marlynn Rosario was born in Burma and came to England when she was three years old, which she says explains elements of her poetry. Her work has been published in various small presses: Iron, London Magazine, Smith's Knoll and Echo Room. She's currently doing the Creative Writing M.A. at the University of Northumbria.

Jane Wood was born in Surbiton but has lived in Newcastle for almost thirty years. She is married with one son, David. She has recently completed an MA in Creative Writing at the University of Northumbria. She has been published in The Page, The Crack and Writing Women.

Jackie Hardy has been writing for about eight years. As well as mainstream poetry, she has an interest in Haiku and edits Blythe Spirit, the Journal of the British Haiku Society. She has had poems published in several magazines including Other Poetry, Writing Women and Poetry Review. Her first collection **Commuting the Waves** is due from Bloodaxe.

Sheila Mulhern hates the Water Board and doesn't know what they're on about.

Debbie Taylor is a writer of fiction, non-fiction and film – and current editor of Mslexia. She has also worked as a researcher-writer for BBC2 and Channel 4, and her drama-documentaries have won several prizes. Her first novel, **The Children Who Sleep By The River** was published by Allison and Busby in 1992. Her second **The Scottish Empress** will be published in 1998.

Heather Young is a retired Community Nursing Sister for Learning Disability and a late starter to writing poetry. She won the 1994 Lace Open Poetry Competition and the 1996 Civil Service Authors Annual Poetry Competition and the 1997 Morpeth Gathering Novice Dialect Competition.

Amanda Thomson graduated from Manchester University with a degree in Creative Arts and an award for 'Most Promising Creative Writer' with votes of fellow students and tutors. She's had work published in 'The Affectionate Punch' and has perfomed in the Green Room in Manchester and Luton Art Centre.